In All Things

By
Mary Thomas

Cover illustration@ by
Su Thomas

Designed 2013 by
One Step Closer Books (OSC)
susanmarytc@gmail.com

Text copyright@ Mary Thomas
Cover illustration copyright@ Su Thomas

All rights reserved; no part of this publication may be reproduced or transmitted by any means, electronic, mechanical, photocopying or otherwise, without the prior permission of the author.

ISBN -13: 978-1482334166

For my children and their families
Susan, Anna and John
Katherine, David, Tim, Holly, Matt and Hope
Peter, Selma, Danny and Isabella
And my brother, John

With love

"In All Things……..."

Was I wrong about everything that day in Florida when I had fasted and prayed? Certainly I seem to have been wrong in one thing. Was I also wrong in this? I felt that God had told me to go ahead with my dream of writing. I returned to England and collected up many of the children's stories I had written. But it did not seem to work out. On the 6th May, 2006, after I had shared my story at a women's worship time two people came to me and said,

"You should write a book".

This has been said to us many times in our lives. Mike's reply had always been that there are too many books on the shelves already. I promised my new friend that I would come home and start. This is it.

The Beginning

Born at the end of the 2nd world war, of which I remember nothing, to older parents, I have often been so grateful in these later years that my mother was a Christian. My father was not although he had been baptised as a young man. As a result she took me to chapel in the morning, Sunday school in the afternoon and back again in the evening. Such was life in the Welsh valleys in those days. I was baptised at the age of 14.

My life was happily spent walking and playing on the mountains, catching tadpoles in the pond, picking primroses and bluebells in those days when one was allowed to do so. My Mum and I would pick the tight buds of sycamore trees in the spring time, bring them home and form wax flowers to decorate their stems. Our best treat was to go up the mountain once a year and take the tent up with us. My much older brother, my Mum, Dad and me. We would light a fire in the hollow of a tree and there have a picnic. I think we played cricket up there also. We played cricket in our back yard; I jumped off the shed and played shops and house in the garage. I took all the local babies for walks in their prams, also in the days when one could do that. Sometimes on Saturdays we would get on the bus and go to a park in the town nearby. We would take a picnic there also. All such simple pleasures but they made up the stuff of a happy childhood.

My brother was my great delight when he was at home, being 12 years older than me. I remember my jealousy when he began to take his girl friends on the back of his motor bike instead of me!

My father was my hero. We would sit in the fire light and play games with the dictionary:

"How do you spell this…?" he would ask.

I love words today. Never underestimate the influence of what parents do with children either for good or for bad.

We would watch what we called "the nuns going to church" which were the red sparks on the soot at the back of the fireplace. We would make patterns in the firelight on the walls. But he was very often sick. When I was engaged and looking forward to being married, I looked forward to the day when I would be able to have him sit in my own garden and be able to take care of him, but that was never to be. He died a few months before our wedding. The shock of that made me break off my engagement. I preferred not to marry than to lose someone else whom I loved. My eager fiancé made sure that that would not be!

Life was not easy for my parents. Being so often ill meant second hand clothes for me except when my mother made me a dress herself. In days before charity shops existed this was not as usual as is was for my own children and grandchildren and for which we are truly happy. Since my father was a miner we would have coal delivered on the back of a lorry a few times a year. I remember how my mother used to go down the garden, fill up the buckets and carry them up to the coal house. My father was unable to help and it gave him great heart-ache to see this. I was never allowed to help though occasionally a neighbour would lend a hand.

My grandmother lived nearby. She was always in pain, and so it is not surprising that I grew up with a fear of sickness, something which God really had to deal with later in my life.

As a child I would apparently teach the flowers! I wonder how I did that? This was my ambition......to be a teacher. Thus it was that I left school to go to college where for three years I trained to teach junior age children.

But the day after I left school I was engaged to Michael, as I called him then. He was the love of my life and was about to start teaching having finished his university career. We had gone to the same school and I had known him as the handsome boy in the sixth form whilst I was very much a junior!

Three years later I graduated and we were married. Then began our adventure! We were so blessed to be able to have our own house straight away since Mike's parents lent us some money as a deposit. We repaid this over the coming years but it had given us a great start.

In the next four and a half years three wonderful children were born to us. Life was great. We sang, we played tennis, Mike played rugby, we enjoyed our children and Mike loved his job. We wished for nothing more. One evening when we were in bed I casually remarked that we were in a rut.

"Yes", Mike agreed.

We concluded that it was a wonderful rut to be in and we wanted nothing else. On that occasion I think the Lord must have had a smile to himself. He knew the plans he had for us. We didn't!

It was not long after this that we discovered that the school Mike was teaching at was intending to become independent. Mike really did not want this and so he began to look for a move. After 8 years of marriage we moved home. How we hated to see the removal van drive away. We had been so happy in this home that it was like bereavement. Now we began a journey which was to take us further than we had ever dreamed both in distance and in experience.

Out of the Depths

We moved from a city to the countryside. It was a perfect time to be in the country whilst our children were young and we were able to enjoy walks through the corn fields and games in the ford. We had no pressure of the children being older and needing to be taken places. But I discovered it to be a very materialistic place. We both had very humble backgrounds. I had lived in a council house and my father had been a miner. Mike had lived in a small house which they owned. His father had been a bus inspector. Here we found ourselves amongst people who had 5 bedroom homes and loved to talk about the extensions they needed.

I remember going to a coffee morning which a friend had kindly arranged so that I could meet my neighbours. I came home in tears because I really had nothing to contribute to the conversation. How on earth was I going to survive in this place?

I did not want to work since Mike and I shared the opinion that a mother's place was in the home. I did not want it to be otherwise although I had loved my teaching job, but I decided eventually to open a nursery school. There were two in the village but both had waiting lists and thus there was room for a third.

In the meantime I took my second daughter to one of the established nursery schools. It was there that I met Susan. It is probably wrong to say I met her. I saw her there each time I took Kathy. We did not exchange many words, but there was something about this woman that I was drawn to.

At this time we were part of a home Bible study group which met in various homes. One evening it was at our home. I answered the door and standing there were some of the usual people, but one of them said,

"I have brought some friends. I hope that's OK!"

Of course, it was Susan and her husband. To say I was surprised would be an understatement.

Even during that first evening I could see such a difference between her and me. She seemed to love reading her Bible. Frankly I found it boring. I had been teaching in Sunday school for years but I only ever read my Bible to prepare for a lesson. And prayer? I prayed in emergency only, but Susan seemed to think it was important and a great thing to do. I had often wondered why my mother- in- law enjoyed reading her Bible so much. I definitely didn't but for the first time in my life I began to question why.

My nursery school had opened with 32 children, two of which were my own two youngest. I loved it. A group of us worked together for no profit to ourselves. We all just simply enjoyed working with the children in these days before Ofsted! But I was becoming more and more discontented with my life.

I went to the doctor's one day to tell him about a spot on my back which was causing me trouble. I went back again some weeks later when that spot had had babies and now covered most of my body. An immediate trip to the hospital for a biopsy told me that it was a quite rare skin complaint. I was prescribed a steroid cream which Mike would rub all over me and then wrap me in polythene each night when we went to bed. Not the best of things! But I began to find myself in tears at the school gate as I waited for my oldest child to come out. I couldn't cope with this. The spots went but I was in despair. I stopped the treatment and the spots reappeared.

All of this coincided with my beginning to cry out to the Lord: "Why is my life so lacking in faith? Have I been playing a game all these years?"

I knew that I needed the rest which the hospital had said was essential, but that would have meant giving up my baby to which I had only just given birth a few years before......the nursery school. I would not do it. The spots persisted.

The Women's World day of prayer arrived. Our speaker was not able to come and so the new vicar of the parish stepped into her place. He preached on "Be still and know that I am God." He used the illustration of traffic lights and put to us the fact that sometimes God shines the red light: it is time to stop and be still. I knew that this was a message from God for me and was one which I could not disobey. On my way home I called in at the home of one of my helpers and asked her if she would be willing to take over the running of the Jack and Jill school after Easter. She was willing. I stopped. My spots disappeared. At last I was being obedient. God had got my attention at last and I was being still. However, I was still crying out for reality in my faith.

One day a friend of mine brought me a library book which she had just read.

"Read this and we can talk about it later", she suggested.

She was herself a nominal Christian. The book was Catherine Marshall's "Beyond Ourselves". I wept as I read and longed to know what it was she was talking about.

I was still attending the weekly home Bible studies although my husband had stopped. One evening, we had just finished the study and were about to start praying when the leader for that evening asked if anyone wanted to say anything. I said that yes, I did want to say something. What followed, I can only ask you to believe. I had never heard of the phrase in my life but I asked, "Please pray that I shall be filled with the Holy Spirit".

Susan was sitting alongside me and immediately said,
"Praise God."

She went on to tell me:

"A few weeks ago I was lowering a child into the swimming pool (she was a physiotherapist for handicapped children) when the Lord told me to pray that Mary would be filled with the Holy Spirit."

"But surely she is already, Lord?"

"Pray that she will be filled," came the command again, and so she did.

And here I was asking!

For weeks I prayed, with no result. What could be wrong? Susan suggested I look at my life to see if there was any unforgiveness in it. Had I, perhaps, hurt someone and needed to ask for their forgiveness? I did find one such thing and promptly went to put it right. Still nothing. I found that I had two disconcerting thoughts. One was that I am Welsh! (The Welsh tend to be more emotional than the English!) I was afraid that I might have an experience which would be just an emotional thing and would vanish out of the window the next day. I was also afraid of what it might do to our marriage. We had such a good marriage, but I instinctively felt that if God moved in my life it might divide us in some way. Susan was again my advisor,

"God created you with your emotions. Let Him do what He will in the way He chooses. As for Mike, leave him to God, and for yourself, be obedient to what He is saying to you."

Thus it was that some nights later I went along to Susan and Brian to ask them to pray for me. Clearly my own prayers were not enough! They prayed. Still nothing. Then Susan suggested that they lay hands on me. They came and stood behind me, put their hands on my shoulders and prayed. Suddenly I stopped them. I had never felt surrounded by such love! It was tangible. It was not their love though I knew I had that. No, this was the love of God. Wonderful! No emotion attached to it at all. Isn't God gracious? I simply said that I longed for a cup of coffee! What do I call this? Was I baptised in the Spirit? Whatever you may choose to call it, it was real.

My life changed in that moment. From that time to this my Bible has become alive to me and prayer has become an essential. That does not mean, however, that I have not had many dry times.

Mike was thrilled that I now became so contented and fulfilled, but he did not wish to change. All was well for him in his own spiritual life. But I now knew that he needed to be filled in the same way that I had been and so I began to pray daily for him.

God spoke to me on one such occasion and made it clear to me that Mike was number one in my life and that that was wrong. God should be first. I struggled with this and took a long time to sort it out. I loved my husband so greatly I did not want him in second place. But God would not be content with that.

Transformation

We were to remain in the countryside for only three years. We had seen an advertisement in the newspaper for a Headship in a place we loved and a school that Mike already knew. Mike applied and was called to interview. However, before that happened, while I was praying one day I knew that God was telling me to ask Him to give us this job, and so I did. I had never done this before!

Previously, at one of the home Bible studies to which I went, the leader prefaced his evening's study with these words:

"As I have been preparing to lead this study I have had a certain verse in my mind which will not go away. It has nothing to do with the study, but I feel compelled to tell you what it is in case it is a verse for one of you here. The verse is John 14 verse 14: "Whatever you ask in My name I will do it."

I could not wait to get home and tell Mike this. No-one at this meeting had been aware of what we were considering.

Mike was one of 12 men called for interview. He visited the local church before going to the school. The Bible was open on the lectern to John chapter 14 and Mike's eyes went immediately to the verse which said,

"Ask and it shall be given to you".

He rang me immediately to tell me this!

A few weeks later he was called to a second interview and this time I was to accompany him. The wife of the Head of our present school told me that I needed to decide what kind of person I wanted to present on this interview day. I went home to ponder this wise advice and realised that it contained no wisdom at all. Praise God that He accepts us just as we are and His plans are for the person we are and shall become in Him, not an idea which we think will please others.

Whilst the men were being interviewed, the Head's wife entertained us by showing us the sights. We were to go to her home for tea but she thought we might just call in the school to see how things were going. Standing in a line in the school yard were the six men who had been interviewed. As we had driven to the school, one of the wives had wondered out loud who would be the successful one. At that moment I could have stood up and said,

"I am so sorry. It's me!"

As we drove in, Mike gave me the tiniest nod of his head. Yes, the job was ours! How thrilled we were. How great is our God!

Eight years followed in this job. For seven of those I prayed every day that Mike would let the Lord into his life. Outwardly he had all the form, as I had done. But inwardly life was becoming tough.

The day came when I told him that I existed to cook his dinner and wash his socks and nothing else. How could this have happened? His job, his hobbies had all taken first place. He became ambitious for the first time in his life. It was an extraordinarily difficult time. I prayed as never before. I played over and over again the record of Mendelssohn's "Elijah", and especially the aria which said "Oh rest in the Lord. Wait patiently for Him and He will give you your heart's desire". Over and over again with tears steaming down my face.

One evening Mike went to speak to a group of men on what it meant to be a Christian and a Headmaster. He took a friend with him in case he dried up because he knew he would be play-acting. I spent the evening with his wife. We drove out to a countryside spot where it was totally dark, and there we prayed and prayed all evening.

On the way home, Mike and his friend stopped to get a drink. As his friend went to the bar to get the drinks Mike had a Damascus road experience. At 10 past 10 on February 13th, 1979 he saw the Lord! He saw the Lord and he saw his own sin and in that moment he was transformed. When we met back at home he told me this but I would not believe him. Three days later, I had gone to bed early but I came back downstairs. Mike was sitting by the fire marking books. As I went into the room he simply said," I wish you would believe me. God has changed me. "I knew it to be true and rushed across the room, throwing myself onto the floor beside him and together we wept for hours. We followed our weeping by praying and praying and then by reading Ephesians which was to become Mike's favourite book. Oh what joy! Thank you, Lord. Now at last I realised that Mike must be second in my life. I knew this because I knew that from now on I wanted to be second in his, not first as I had always wished. No. If I became second to God, then I would be in my rightful place and the same for me with him. God would be our very best guide.

We were helped so much during this time by two friends of ours, a husband and wife. I have heard it said often that one should not interfere in others marriage problems. I believe that to be so wrong. Had these two not intervened and helped us individually and together, who knows what would have happened. They saw that we had problems and because they loved us and knew the power of God they set about helping trusting God to answer their fasting prayers. How I have thanked God for these two.

There were times in the years which followed when I found I needed to check up that God was still first. I never wanted it to change.

God used this dreadful time in our lives for His very own purposes. I will go further and say that He allowed it all to happen in order that we would see just how much we needed God to be the Head of our home and how much we needed to have our own individual relationship with Jesus.

"In all these things God works for the good of those who love Him who are called according to His purpose".

I can truly say that I would have gone through all of that again in order to discover the joy and future that God had in store for us.

During this time I had learned the power in the name of Jesus. An elderly friend told me how helpful I would find it to simply call out His name. There had been times when I did not have words to pray. He heard my groaning and the many times I would just repeat His name over and over again, only to need to do it again five minutes later. What great things these are to learn, but I think we can only learn them in the difficult times when we are weak and have to rely on His strength. He is faithful. He hears our prayers.

Some weeks later we were sitting by the fire reading …..guess what?...Ephesians. As we finished reading and just sat there quietly, Mike suddenly said, "I don't think you are going to believe what God has just said to me."

He put his Bible up in front of his face as I asked what it was.

"I believe He is calling us to full time ministry!"

I have often been asked what on earth my reaction was to that stunning statement. It was this:

"I feel that God has been preparing me for this all of my life."

I had never thought of it but I knew it to be true.

We excitedly shared this with two pastor friends of ours. We expected that we would hear from them quickly since they would be as excited as we were. But no. The first one waited several weeks and then called us.

"I wanted to give you time to let the novelty of the idea wear off".

We told him that it had not done that and so he rejoiced with us. The second we told face to face. He looked at us with his ever piercing eyes and simply said

"Don't do it."

What was wrong with this man? He continued,

"Don't do it unless you are absolutely sure that this is the call of God. If it is, when the dark moments come you will be able to remember that you were called. If not, you will have great doubts and life will be so miserable."

What words of wisdom these were. How rightly both men reacted to our news. We did know that God had called us.

In the months which followed we investigated ways of training for ministry and were shown that Mike could do an external theology degree. And so began mornings of getting up at 5.00am to study, off to school, home and games with the children, school work and then study late into the night.

Our young son told his friend that Dad was re-writing the Bible! It was not an easy time. There were moments when I was so fed up with our not being able to spend time together. Moments when we almost decided to give it all up. Amazingly, Mike was asked if he would like a sabbatical three months during the coming school year. He delightedly said that he would and chose to take it from Easter until the summer, hence giving him plenty of time before his exams in July. No-one was aware of the preparation for ministry that we were making! Yet again, all things were working together to fulfil God's purposes. Two years after beginning, all was completed and Mike had gained his Diploma in Theology

Another important thing happened while we were living here and going through this tough time. My mother was diagnosed with having cancer. I was terrified especially when she was given a mere 6 weeks to live. She came to live with us in September and until Christmas made enormous effort to keep going. Late on Christmas day she took to her bed and stayed there. Already the six weeks had long passed.

For years I had shared the verse "I can do all things through Christ who strengthens me" with many people and assured them of the truth of this verse. Now it seemed that God was saying to me," You have believed this verse for other people, now will you believe it for yourself?"

I would walk along to her bedroom, not sure what I would find and as I walked I would say to myself," I CAN do ALL things......" Incidentally, this is a wonderful way to meditate on God's word......simply choose a verse and repeat it until you have emphasised each word in turn. The meaning is different each time!

A wonderful thing had happened the day my mother had arrived in our home. The evening before, I had been getting her bedroom ready. My brother was bringing all her homely things with him, including all her bedding, and so the room was empty. A full moon shone through the window. I stood by the window and cried out to God for His help. I asked Him to fill the room with His presence and to bless Mum's being there.

When she eventually managed to get to her room I opened the door. In the short while since her arrival my sister-in-law and I had hung pictures, made the bed, put plants around and generally made it look like home for her. As she went in she gasped. That was all, and then slept for some hours. When she awoke her comment was, "As you opened the door and I looked inside I felt that I was seeing a glimpse of heaven."

She told everyone who visited about this experience. Surely God had answered my prayer!

She lived for 6 months during which time the Lord did many wonderful things.

It was not an easy time, but it WAS possible. My friend Liz was the angel God used to help me. I saw that Jesus needed an angel to minister to him in the garden of Gethsemane. If he needed an angel, then how much more did I? If only we could all learn to minister to each other in the gentle way she ministered to me.

God used these two verses, Romans 8:28 and Philippians 4:13 to show me that He always keeps His promises. Little did I know how important the nursing of my mother would prove to be in my later life. I was to discover that even in this God would work for my good because I loved Him.

I learned a hard truth many years later, when I was teaching a Korean post graduate at the university to write English for his essays. In one of our conversations he told me of a Korean saying: Downward love is much greater than upward love", referring to the love of parents for their children. Of course, it also applies to God. How I wish it had been possible to learn these lessons earlier in life. I so regret now that my relationship with my Mum was far less than it could have been, and that was my fault. I was not as caring as I should have been, or as loving. I am so sorry. How can one teach this to the next generation? I wish it were possible. They are not good regrets to live with. I look forward to meeting her in heaven and asking her forgiveness.

Out of our Comfort Zone

Mike was now qualified, what next? We had expected and indeed, been told, that after this Mike would be given a church, but this was not to be. Mike had not trained in the normal acceptable way and apparently this made things difficult. We had no idea what we were going to do but God had it in hand, far more wonderfully than we could have ever imagined.

We gave hospitality to the then head of evangelism for the Baptist Union who had recently travelled to the USA to discover what was causing the church in America to grow whilst the church in Britain was losing people. He was full of his adventure there and talked of one church in California in particular. Some months later we repeated this hospitality and on this occasion he brought photographs to show us.

At tea times in our home we would often play the game "If you could go anywhere in the world where would you choose to go?" I remember that bottom of my list came America and Russia! As Lewis showed us his photographs and as we shared with him the call God had given us to the ministry, a plan began to form in our minds. Might it be a good idea for us to go to the States and see for this growth for ourselves? Several times we had exchanged homes for holidays. Would it be possible to do this in California? We had never even considered such an adventure before.

We wrote to the pastor of the church asking if he thought anyone in his congregation (of 3500!) would like a holiday in Britain. Before too long we heard that, yes, there was such a family. Planning for a holiday in America was beyond our wildest dreams and with three children now aged 15, 13 and 11 the excitement was extreme!

Years before, my Mum had given us some money after the death of her brother, in the form of some kind of bonds. We had put it away and literally forgotten about it. As we tidied a cupboard one day I came across the folder with them in. The money had increased, of course, and was the exact amount needed for the fare for all 5 of us to the States!

The reason I had never wanted to go to the States was because I imagined it to be all sky scrapers, noise and shallow people. Where did I get all that from? Now we found ourselves making these plans. A family with two boys would come and live in our home and we would go to theirs. We wrote to the senior pastor asking him if it would be possible for us to join in the life of the church whilst we were there.

In August we set off for four weeks. It was the first time the children had flown. What an adventure. Our rut had certainly disappeared! How amazingly God orchestrates things. Had we not given hospitality to these folk who had been strangers to us, we would never have been doing this!

We met our American friends in the home of some friends of ours in London. They drove off in our car……the wrong side of the road. We felt we would never see that car again! When we arrived in California we had moments of panic as we realised what we would have to drive through. But we made it and found ourselves in a beautiful cedar- wood Californian home.

Almost immediately we were contacted by one of the 23 pastors in the church inviting us to go to their home. And so began the most wonderful month we had ever had. We felt that God multiplied the weeks since we had both a wonderful time being involved fully in the church where we were welcomed so warmly and were also given amazing hospitality, and saw the sights of California: Yosemite, Tahoe, Disney Land, Universal Studios, Carmel and so much more. We saw racoons, chipmunks, gophers, pelicans and seals. God gave to us pressed down and flowing over in every way. How different from my imagination was this California! We saw such beauty, we experienced such stillness in amongst the wonders of His stunning creation and we had to be on our knees asking for forgiveness about our harsh judgement of the people.

On the last day of our visit we shared with the children the fact that we would be leaving the school at the end of the following year and going into ministry.

"Can we do it here?" asked Pete.

"No, this is a one-off," was our reply.

And home we went.

This church had an international ministry. It had around 40 interns, some from New Zealand and Singapore. In November of the same year Mike came up with the idea of our going there to study. "How on earth can we do that?" I asked. "Susan is about to go into her last year at school ,preparing for her A-level exams; Kathy is just about to begin her O level course and Pete is about to go to secondary school. We can't possible disrupt their lives at this time". We talked and prayed and eventually decided that it was right to ask if it might be possible for us to go there. I found that if I looked at the problem of schooling then I was lost. If I kept my eyes on the Lord all was well.

One evening in November Mike had arranged to call Pastor Yeager. As he spoke on the phone I waited with the children in the living room. We were all pretending that it didn't matter! He came in,

"We're going" he exclaimed, "for three years!"

I don't think any of us slept that night. We would leave on July 28th.

We would not be earning any money whilst we were there since we were to be students. The church had said they would take us only as long as both of agreed to be trained. How wonderful that was.

The morning after this telephone call to the States there came a call to our home. A stranger to me said that he would like to offer Mike an assistant pastorate on the recommendation of a mutual friend but had heard that we were considering going to California. I told him that we had made a decision only the night before. I called Mike at school to tell him of this call and he said he would come home straight away so that we could discuss it. Whilst I waited for him to arrive I took a piece of paper, divided it down the middle and wrote "Advantages" on one side and "Disadvantages" on the other.

The attractions and advantages of taking this pastorate were great. A lovely place to live, a house with the job, good schools for the children near to Mike's ageing parents. On the disadvantage side was going to America! No salary, where would we live, far away from Mike's parents, an entirely different schooling system for the children, and so on, endlessly. Mike and I talked only briefly.

"We have made a decision," Mike said, "we must stick to it."

The decision was made and so we decided we would start to live simply even at this stage. Out went chocolate, orange juice, butter, chocolate biscuits, steak. We all happily agreed that this was a good thing to do. What wonderful support our children were in these things. It was going to be a great experience! We saved a lot of money in those months and in July we were ready.

We were often asked how we could give up such a good job, a lovely house, a lovely place to live, a salary and security in order to go to a strange place and live there with no income. Why would Mike choose to give up being a Headmaster, a job where he could have such influence? Mike's reply to the latter was that as Head he was actually limited in what he could say and do in Christian terms. As for giving up the rest we really did not feel we were giving up anything because we were so sure that this was the plan God had for us all. We did not make a choice in fact. It was clear that this is what we should do and so we were doing it.

It is no good looking at someone else and saying "I could never do that. What faith you have." We could only do it because God had called us to do so. It would have been much harder not to do it.

How blessed we were. Mike was an only child of elderly parents. But they loved the Lord. Never once did we receive any word of disappointment or recrimination. As we left them, not knowing if we would see them again, they sent us off with smiles and their blessing. God blessed them with many years of life and so we did have a future together. But at this point we did not know that. I learned from them at this time what I would later determine to put into practise with my own children. I hope I have.

Our furniture was put into store in the chapel that Mike's parents attended. The night before we were due to leave we received a phone call giving us the address at which we would be living. At last! Up until that point we had no idea where we were going! Our bags were packed and on July 28th friends took us to the airport. Friends and family arrived unexpectedly to say goodbye to us. One pair waved a banner saying

"Come back. Britain needs you! "

A new life was about to begin.

Pastures New

Our home in California was almost smaller than the sitting room in the house we had left behind! In their late teens our daughters had to adjust to bunk beds instead of their individual bedrooms. The entire house had been furnished for us by donations from various people. Everything matched! How gracious God is!

How wonderful it was for Mike and me to see our children singing with the choir on a Sunday evening. About 200 young people stood and sang, praising the Lord. In England they had almost been the only Christians in their peer groups. I believe we wept with joy the first time we saw the girls singing up there. They were both in the High School whilst Peter was in Junior High and had his own equivalent vibrant group.

Each school had a member of staff from the church working at the school in order to be on hand for anyone who wanted to talk to them at any time. I remember Peter school- refusing one day because he was afraid of the PE teacher and his hooked hand. It was so great to be able to call this staff member for help. What a blessing. I know that this is now happening in this country at last. If only all our schools and churches here could have such a vision. Life would be so much easier for many students.

Our plan was for Susan to continue her last year of British education whilst we were in the States. She would drop one of her A level subjects, Mike would then teach her Latin and I would do her English. Mike had already arranged with the Cambridge Board that she would be allowed to take the exams there in the US at the end of that school year. However, we very quickly realised that if Susan was to take full advantage of living in the States, and especially of being part of such a vibrant church, then there was going to be too little time for her to also continue her studies for "A" level. We prayed and sought wisdom and then together decided that we would trust God in this and allow her to drop these subjects.

We allowed ourselves just $5 a week for gas for the car……..which had been given to us. When we had used up that gas we relied on our bikes which we had shipped over. The children rode on theirs to school each day.

I remember especially, one day when I was discipling three senior girls at my home. We were studying the book" What happens when women pray" by Evelyn Christenson. A phone call interrupted our session. Susan spoke,

"Our bikes have been stolen, all three. We have looked everywhere and cannot find them."

I told them I would call Dad at the church and we would get in touch with the police. In the meantime, told them to go on looking! It then occurred to me that this fitted so well with what we were studying and so together the four of us prayed that the Lord would find these all important bikes.

A short while later the phone rang again. This time it was the police, "We have just had two bikes brought into the station. Would you like to come down and see if they are yours?"

We jumped into the car and raced to the station. Yes, these two were ours! The police told us that someone had just brought them in and left them and quickly gone away. They had no name.

"Does this happen very often?" we asked.

"Never," was the reply.

I remember hugging the policeman! But where was the third?

I was meandering down the corridor along which were several bikes which had been found in various places. There was Peter's bike! We often say that we should not be amazed that God answers prayer. But I think it would be a sad day when such a happening would fail to amaze us. How great and wonderful is our God!

Our lives in California were littered with miracles. We had discovered to our dismay that whilst our children had worn school uniform in Britain here in America it was a fashion show each day. Girls, boys, too, would wear something different every day. How were we going to handle this one? We had bought clothes before we left Britain, but it was not going to enable the girls to compete with this life style. What were we to do? Should we take some of our savings and buy more for them? Should we say we were simply not going to join in this way of life? We prayed about it and waited to hear what we should do.

One morning I was at Bible study. One of the pastors came into the room just before we were about to begin. He was nicknamed "Pastor Disaster" because he was the one who dealt with all pastoral matters. He came to me, "Mary, would you come and see me afterwards?"

I found it difficult to concentrate on the study. What can have gone wrong that this pastor needed to speak to me? I went to his room afterwards and he asked me if I had my car with me. I did. He took me into his office and there on the floor were brown paper bags galore.

"The college girls have gone through their closets and found clothes that they are not wearing. They want to give them to your girls as a gift!"

It took my car and his to take them to our home. There I placed them all over the floor just as I had first seen them and we waited for the girls to come home. What lovely clothes were in these bags. God gave to us abundantly more than all we could have asked or imagined.

Not once during our time in Modesto did we make a need known since we had undertaken to be self-supporting before we came. We relied on money coming monthly from the UK. It totalled £3000 a year, not a great deal even in 1980. One month it did not come. We shared this with the children wanting them to be aware of such things. We prayed together. All was well because my store cupboard fed us. But it did not come the second month, either.

"How is God going to do this for us?" asked Peter, excitedly, believing that He would.

The third month still brought no cheque. By now our cupboard was bare.

And so it was that a knock came at the door. We went to answer it and found no-one there. We went round to the drive way and there on the bonnet of our car was a cardboard box. We never discovered who had put it there. It was full of cuts of beef. Our freezer was a small one at the top of our fridge. Not all of it would fit in!

And what about the couple who told us on that Sunday morning that they would like to supply us with eggs for our duration in the States from their chicken farm? Each Sunday after that they brought us a tray of 30 eggs!

Then Ben brought us 2 gallons of milk, straight from the cows. Each Sunday we collected milk from him and eggs from the Gervase's.

But what had happened to our money? After this third month and many phone calls to the bank in Britain, we established that it had been sent to the wrong branch in Modesto. It had been there all the time! What we would have missed of God's generosity to us if we had known that from the beginning!

Like Ruth we learned to glean………..peaches, tomatoes, walnuts, almonds and I learned to can. Another friend had invited us to dine at their home and during the meal when we were eating the biggest T- bone steaks we have ever seen, from their own cows, they told us that they would like to supply us with beef for the duration of our stay in America. How amazed the Lord kept us! What wonderful lessons in being generous we were learning.

Just before we had left for the States the Lord had given me three verses in preparation for our going. One was Malachi 3:10:

"Bring your full tithe into the store house and see if I will not open the windows of heaven and pour out so much blessing that you will not be able to contain it,"

We were living the truth of that verse.

The second was Matthew

"Seek first the kingdom of God and his righteousness and all these things will be added unto you."

One morning I was sitting on the patio under the veranda reading my Bible when the Lord gave me a verse I wished he had not given, Luke 12:48:

"From those to whom much is given, much will be required."

My word, no-one could be receiving more than we were.

"Lord, what are you going to require?" I asked fearfully.

Only He knows the answer to that question. Sometimes I have found myself thinking

"Oh, this is what he requires of us" when hard moments have come.

But I cannot honestly say that I know which has been which or if more will come. I have a feeling they will. But maybe the much that He is demanding is simply that we should be obedient disciples. Simply?

His bounty continued. One evening as we left a home we were given an envelope "to help us with our daily living." I counted out the notes in the darkness of the car as we drove home that night. There were 10 of them, $100. What a great gift. When we got home we discovered $1000 in that envelope, not $100.

We were given a weekend in a cabin in the mountains. A snow blizzard fell to our wonder as we watched at the top of pine tree level. We lay on a chaise langue before a roaring log fire and made love before this beautiful scene. What could be more perfect?

We were walking by the lake the next day when we realised we had left our camera back in the valley. We met a stranger and shared our thoughts on the beauty of the scene.

"Take my camera," he said. "Bring it back to me tomorrow."

Not just an old cheap camera, but an expensive one! How overwhelming was this generosity. Maybe he was an angel.

Even as I write these words my heart thrills within me at the remembrance of all these happenings. What a great experience God was giving us. Our lives were changed for ever as we lived in this great land.

Our children were given a foundation built upon rock during these years. Our son was to find a youth leader who became a great friend whom I believe saved his life at a much later stage. All of them and Mike and I, were being taught to apply the Word of God to all aspects of our living. These lessons have never deserted us.

At the end of two years there Mike was offered a pastor's job in the church. How we longed to take it. However, Mike was fully convinced that we had gone to the States to be trained in ministry in order to come back to the UK. And so it was that we found ourselves at San Francisco airport in August of 1984, on the way back to Britain.

A month or two earlier Mike had called some of our friends who lived in London which is where he believed we were being called to minister.

"Would you be able to buy a car for us and find us a house to live in, please?"

It is fun to hear them relate this story. They had never done such a thing for anyone. Few have! But they set about the task and they, too, discovered how mighty our God is as He supplies all our need. This was the same angel who had ministered to me when my Mum was sick. We arrived back on August 18th and there was our car waiting to take us to our rented home.

Before we had left America the senior pastor had asked how much it was going to cost us to rent this house. There and then he had written out a cheque for 6 months rent. What can I say!

"We have not trained you thus far without being willing to support you until you can do it for yourselves," was his gracious comment.

of the six months since that was the contract we had with him. We did not know how to answer him. We were no nearer finding a church, but how much longer should we be prepared to stay in this house? Also, the money we had received from our church in America covered six months only. We were concerned.

Mike was out one evening when the phone rang and an American voice spoke to me.

"How are you doing for money?" were the first words Pastor Yeager said.

I hesitated for a moment and then told him what was happening, or not happening.

"I will put a cheque into the post tomorrow for a further three months," he said.

And so he did.

It is so easy just to report all these things happening as if they were common place. Perhaps they should be, after all, we serve a God who "owns all the cattle on a thousand hills." Watchman Nee writes in his book "The Normal Christian Life" that we should live a naturally supernatural life. This is what we were doing. Every step of the way God showed Himself to be there with us. In every situation He had already prepared the way. In all these things He worked for the good of we who loved Him. Every moment which threatened to be troublesome He allowed for a while and then released us. He never gave us more than we were able to deal with and each time He showed us how to stand up under the difficulties. We were discovering the truth of that fact that God is just plain wonderful! The truth of 1 Corinthians 10:13 was proved to us over and over again.

The moment came when invitations began to arrive asking Mike to preach. This was such an arduous task. We often travelled long distances to these churches. One asked us rather quickly to take the pastorate. We were so reluctant. This would definitely mean that we would have to move the children at a really difficult stage of their schooling again and we had asked God not to let this happen. However the church was insistent that they felt this was God's plan. The deacons were unanimous and so Mike went to preach with a view to the pastorate. We had had a heavy snowfall and so we decided that Mike would go by himself on the train. How he wished I had been there with him. He always hated preaching when I was not there in the congregation.

This church was way down south. Another, out towards the east coast also issued an invitation to the pastorate, and all the while, the one we had thought would be the church we would go to had still not made up its mind.

We did not know what to do. The call to two churches was clear. The third, from which we had not heard, was the only one which would mean that the children would not have to move schools. Mike gave them an ultimatum, however, which resulted in our withdrawing. At the same time another church invited us to go to preach there one Sunday. It was not too far away and the children accompanied us for the morning service. It was so cold following another snow storm.

Few were in this service. We had not accepted hospitality because we felt it important just to be together as just a family at this trying time. Mike and I went back to the evening service on our own. At the end of the evening service the church secretary came to us and said that he had contacted all church members that afternoon and they would like us to go and meet their selection committee. Mike explained that we could not do that since he was considering a call to another church. We eventually agreed to go if they would consider it practise for us at this other church! They agreed!

What should we do? We read Acts 16 and felt that as a result of reading this that we should ask God to close two of the doors. A few nights later we had a call from the first church telling us that because Mike was not an accredited Baptist pastor their deeds would not allow him to go to them. However, they were considering changing their constitution to allow it! Mike said that they should not do this since it would cause a split in the church. One door was closed.

The second church was very far away and although we had loved being there and had been given great hospitality, we felt that it did not fit with what we had asked of God and thus we felt it right to withdraw. That left only the one we had gone to practise on. Not our favourite. Mike called them to tell them that they had not realised he was not an accredited Baptist pastor and that therefore, they would not be able to call him. Their reply was that they had rarely had one who was accredited.

Thus it was that we became the pastors of this church. Where was it? A walk along the road from where Peter went to school and a single bus ride for Kathie to her college. Oh, my breath is taken away as I write this. How amazingly incredible is our God!

This period had been the hardest time for us, but also provided the best training for the future. We had had to learn to rely on God alone and to trust him for the future. We did not always have the faith we should have had. It was a struggle, but as a pastor recently said to me, "A struggle shows that you are alive. If there were no struggle we would be dead!"

Years of Plenty

We began our pastorate on June 1st, 1985. "The glorious first of June" as it was always referred to by one of our elderly church members whose greatest interest was history. I still cannot remember what battle and victory it referred to!

The church was too small to give us much of a salary and because we were not accredited they could not seek help from the Baptist Union. By faith we agreed to receive it saying that we had lived on less for the past three years.

What a sense of humour the Lord has. We had been trained in a church of 3500. We were now in a church which had 37 active members only. Our Sunday School class in America had numbered 120!

Mike and I began by leading small groups several days of the week. He and I both led small discipleship groups. Together we began an evangelism class with just two other members and later these groups expanded to include a couples group, marriage classes, women's Bible studies and early morning studies for the men. We were busy but greatly blessed. The church began to grow and we were thrilled to see some of the members rededicate their lives to the Lord and others come to faith for the first time. What can be more exciting!

I must recall an incident which happened early on. I had been praying that the Lord would lead me to women who wanted to grow in the Lord as much as I did. The day after our induction Mike asked me to go and visit an elderly lady who had just come out of hospital. I did so and towards the end of my visit she told me that at the age of 83 she was ashamed to say that she did not know how to pray. I knew this was the moment I had prayed for. I asked her if she would like me to visit her the following week with the express purpose of teaching her to pray. She did not hesitate to say yes and said that her daughter-in –law with whom she lived would probably come, too. Anne was not a Christian so I doubted if she would.

The following week I went along only to find four people waiting for me to arrive! I had suggested we did a Bible study as well as pray and this was the beginning of one of the most exciting things in our church … women's Bible studies.

Some while later, when we all knew each other very well, and the group had grown to around 12 women aged from 30 to 90, there came a moment when Anne asked me if I would call later that night to talk to her about becoming a Christian. I had had several conversations with her along these lines but always she had said that later would do. I replied that I would certainly come that evening but why wait until then? Why not talk about it there and then with the group present. We did. The result was that Anne gave her life to the Lord and has been a radiant Christian ever since with great gifts for hospitality and evangelism. This was wonderful because only a few weeks into our ministry her husband had come to see us early one morning and had received Jesus at our breakfast table. So many tears were wept, all of joy.

There were so many lovely moments but I will allow myself just one more! One Sunday morning a lady in her 50's spoke to us on the way out of church:

"I am never coming here again," she said. "You are always telling me things I do not want to hear. I am so angry."

We had a good relationship with this lady, so far, anyway. She was a lovely knitter and I was unable to knit very much at all and so, some weeks later I asked her if I could go and spend one evening with her so that she could show me how to do it! She happily agreed to this and during the evening we listened to music that we both loved. Just as I said it was time for me to be going home, Florrie said, "I have been so miserable ever since you came to this church. I was happy before."

I asked her if she would allow me to pray for her and she agreed. I was given real boldness as I closed my prayer with the words

"Lord, keep Florrie miserable until she comes to know you fully."

I wonder how I got out of there safely!

Christmas day dawned a few weeks after this. Our first Christmas in this church. Mike preached and afterwards asked "Is there anyone who would like to give their lives to the Lord today. What a wonderful day it would be to begin a Christian life." We had an agreement between us that if ever anyone did accept the Lord and walk to the front of the church then I or one of the few we were so far training would accompany them so that they would not feel too isolated. We began to sing our last carol during which Mike had asked anyone to come forward if they so wished. After just one verse he gave me an imperceptible nod of his head. This should mean that I should go forward with someone, but that could not be so. I could not think of anyone who would do this. I turned to see if anyone was coming down the aisle. Yes. Florrie was. I joined her and we wept together at the front of the church. "I have given you a hard time" she said. But what a reward. Florrie went on later to lead one of our women's Bible study groups. She was not destined to live for too long but is now in the right place with her Lord.

Mike and I worked as a team and loved every moment of it. Our salary quickly grew and eventually the giving stretched to include a youth pastor, a student pastor and a church house for the elderly. Purses were released, a sure sign of growth in the Lord. We pastored many people who were so faithful to the Lord and in their care and love for us. They have remained so to this very day.

The nine years we ministered in this place were blessed indeed. We saw our nest empty as our children went off to nurse and to university. But it was quickly filled by Mike's parents coming to live with us. They had lived in their home for 56 years but they left it quietly and calmly with no regrets that they communicated to us. They knew they would be coming to a new church family, and that for them was so important. They could not have been better parents- in -law for me, but it was not an easy time. I had cause to regret so many things in terms of my actions and thoughts when seven years later they had both died. It took some while to deal with the guilt I felt about my behaviour. They were so grateful to have a home with us and I trust that many of their days there were happy ones.

They celebrated their 60th wedding anniversary whilst with us, a cause for great celebration which Mike and I both missed since our first grandchild chose that moment to be born and we raced up the motor way to be there when he arrived. Gran's parents before them had also celebrated their 60th anniversary and so we boast two telegrams from the Queen! Maybe we would have one ourselves one day!

We had been in the church for 8 years when one Thursday morning found me ironing in the kitchen. As I ironed the Lord spoke to me:

"Your time in this place is coming to an end", He said.

How do we know God is talking to us? I find this difficult to explain. You just know in your spirit. Forgive me for not being clearer. I argued with Him, "It can't be," I said. "We are training a student pastor for one more year after this one. We cannot move our parents again at their age and thirdly, our daughter and her family are living nearby for another year whilst they train for mission."

There would be no way we could move at this time. I said nothing to Mike and so dismissed it.

After church on the following Sunday evening we were sitting eating our sandwiches when suddenly Mike said

" I think our time in this place is coming to an end."

"Why do you say that?" I asked, amazed.

"I don't know. I just feel in my spirit that that is what God is saying."

You can guess the conversation which followed!

We decided we would say nothing to anyone for a while and just wait to see if it was confirmed in some way. Eventually we shared it with the deacons and said that we would leave at the end of one more year with them.

During that year Gran died. The college our son-in-law attended decide to close and re-open in another county far away. Our student pastor said that he would like to have just one year in a college. All these things God knew as He had spoken to me on that Thursday morning, and I had thought He was being unreasonable. "In all these things.........."

We knew that He had also told us that we were to leave regardless of whether we had anything to go to or not.

At the end of that period, we had nothing to go to ………..again!

"I do love to be beside the sea-side!"

When Mike's parents had moved to live with us they had insisted that we took the small amount of money they had received for their house. We had eventually agree to do this and bought a house near the sea on the south coast. Mike had often said to me, "One day I will take you to live by the sea."

This was my dream! During our ministry years we had taken advantage of staying there as often as we could and had no need of holidays elsewhere. It was also a lovely place to be able to take Mike's parents for a break. And so when the year ended we took ourselves off to the sea-side. Grampa in tow with us!

We knew that this was not retirement, which many had assumed it was. But what could be next we had no idea. Mike was not one to enjoy sitting on the patio day after day however many books he was now free to read, and he began to be restless. I simply enjoyed the walks by the sea!

In the year whilst we had been preparing to leave the church we had received a call from a pastor friend of ours in Florida. He had told us that they had a problem in their church which they thought we might be able to help with. Our church had given us time off to go over and see if we could do so. I don't recall that we were able to do anything significant, but whilst we were there Mike met the man who was heading up their mission team in the church. He told Mike of a vision he had of someone coming to help them to lead the church forward in mission. As they talked he had broken down and said that he felt Mike might be that man. They agreed to pray about it and to seek confirmation of whether this was to be or not.

So it was not a total surprise when the day came that we received another call to ask us if we would go over to lead and build up a mission department in this church.

Grampa had had a stroke which had recently meant that he had to be cared for in a home. It was he who had said that he must do this because he realised it would be too difficult to look after him at home. But this was one of the most painful things we were ever called to do. So many of these places are not fit to be called "homes" and I felt guilty that I was not now looking after him although we truly felt that it was not possible to met his needs. Doctors agreed with us and indeed, Grampa was the first to say that I could not and that he must go into a home. He was always selfless. The pastor of his old home church asked if he could be moved to a home near them so that his church could care for this man they had loved for so many years. For him it was a return to his beloved Wales. As we drove into the car park I remember him saying,

"I am home!"

Thus we were free to accept this call and move to Florida.

We stayed there for three wonderful years during which time we had thought we might even decide to live permanently in this place we had grown to love. We received no salary but again were able to work as a team. We were mightily blessed during these years.

One of the things we have always received has been God's gift of faithful friends. How precious did these East coast American friends become and how precious they have remained. God had certainly planted our feet in beautiful places with beautiful people.

I wish I could say that our time there was successful in building up a great mission work in this church. It was not although it was a beginning. But it was a great time for teaching us many new things which were to prepare us for yet another different future.

Another future? A different one? Surely that is not possible!

Far-away Land

We left Florida on Easter Monday, returning to our sea-side home. Again we had no idea what would come next. The word "retired" in no sense of the word could be used to describe how we felt about what future we had before us. What it was to be we would never have guessed.

Before these things could come to pass, however, there were immediate family things to take care of. We had been home only for a few weeks when we received a phone call to tell us that Mike's Dad had just been rushed to hospital and that it was unlikely that he would live. Leaving me to contact the rest of the family, Mike quickly left to go to be with his Dad. He did not die then and we were granted weeks of joy with him.

The day after Mike had left the phone rang at lunch time. It was our son calling to tell us that his wife had left him. This was a great shock although it came at the end of several very difficult years which had greatly grieved our hearts.

We had thought of maybe staying in Florida for ever. The Lord had made it clear to us that we should go home. For either of the above events we would have to have come home. How gracious it was that God already had us there.

And so it was that the world's best Grampa died a few months later, and we found ourselves coping with the fact that our son was now on his own and was eventually divorced. Such things only happened in other families.

As a family we had to come to terms with what this meant. We believed God's word implicitly and know that He hates divorce. Yet this is what had happened. We all struggled with this in our own way but for Mike and me it was the beginning of a realisation that God's grace far outstrips ours. His love and mercy are indeed new every morning. We knew that our task was to give our son our unconditional support through all of this and to trust God to take us on.

Years later, a few hours before his marriage to a wonderful girl, he broke down when talking to us. I wondered what was causing his tears but we let him simply cry as we held him close. When his tears were spent, he said,

"I cannot believe that God is so gracious as to let me have another go."

Such is our God. He and his family minister to street boys and communities in north eastern Brazil, a calling that had been on his life since the age of 14. But all of that is his story! What pain and joy is ours in abundance as we share life with our children.

Somewhere along here Mike received a call from a mission of which he was a director. He had often tried to resign from this post since we were not in the country and he was not fulfilling any of the responsibilities of a director. His resignation was never accepted since the Board said that he was the only one of them actually doing mission! How interwoven are God's plans for our lives. How complicated the thread. This position had come about as a result of those years in California. Now God's next plan for our lives was to come into being.

Years before when we had been pastoring the church, every time we had a mission speaker Mike would always end the evening with his arm around their shoulders and would say,

"This is wonderful work. I would love to be coming to do it with you!"

It became a predictable moment the whole church would wait for!
I knew that there was more than a little truth in what Mike was saying and it was always with some trepidation that I waited for him to say it.

"Would you go to Mexico and Guatemala for us to see how the work is going there?"

How could he refuse after so many years of doing nothing? The plan was that Mike would go on his own since we had no idea what such work entailed. We knew it would be no joy ride since he would be visiting some of the poorest places in the world. Armed with Imodium and goodness knows what else, Mike set off.

For the first time in our lives we were to be separated. Not something we welcomed or ever enjoyed. Thank God for the computer which enabled us to email each other many times a day over the next years if it was possible to do so.

Mike returned from this trip having lost his heart to Guatemala. It was not enough for him to simply go to visit to see if all was going well. He felt that in order to really understand how things were going then it was necessary to go and be there with the people, to live with them and get to know them. And so it was not very long before another trip to Guatemala was arranged and on this occasion I was to fly out to join him there.

Many commented on how brave we were to do this. The truth? Mike was excited but I was scared stiff. Often Mike would ask me,

"Where is your sense of adventure?"

I would always reply that I did not have one! I went as a willing helper to my husband. I do not like dirt and smells. I did not think I would cope with third world living, but I wanted to be with Mike and he wanted us to do this together and so after he had been there a few weeks I flew out via Los Angeles to join him.

I had a wait of eight hours at Los Angeles airport, a long time to contemplate a journey which would take me to such a different land. Not long before it was time to board the plane, as I was talking to a Philippine lady, we were looking at a man who was sitting in a wheel chair.

"That man does not have long to live", said my companion.

I agreed with her. Imagine my utter horror when I boarded the plane to find that my seat was next to this man. There was nothing I could do about it since the plane was obviously bursting at the seams. So sit there I did. He was very unwell during the journey and I wondered if I was being given an insight into the kind of things I was going to experience in this strange land.

Mike had told me to get a window seat so that I might be able to see the volcanoes surrounding Guatemala City, some of which were still active. I was not at all sure

I really wanted to see volcanoes, but I was an obedient wife.

Mike had been very fulsome in his praise of the work he had visited in Guatemala City. A school had been started 50 years before to cater for those who would otherwise not be able to afford to go to school. He had not exaggerated. To be with these people and to share a little in their work was the most wonderful thing. The school now had several thousand pupils, some of them being taught through distance learning. What a privilege it was to teach the children English at the primary school.

We went to an assembly in the senior school, a crowd of several hundred pupils. It was a wonderfully joyous experience. At the end of the "service" the leader called a young girl to the front. He explained how the family of this girl were having a very difficult time financially and he asked for the prayers of the school. He then said that prayers were no good unless we were also willing to do something about it and he asked who from amongst the pupils would be willing to covenant a small amount to this family each week for the next year. There was no pause as many surged forward. The leader commented, "Today you have had a share in the kingdom of God. Would you not like your children to be a part of such a school?" He had taught that we need to put legs on our prayers.

How amazing it was to receive the love of these people so freely. We saw great poverty, great need. I was glad I was there and it changed my life. I saw so clearly when we came home how very rich we are as a nation and how dissatisfied.

A number of years before this we had been in Poland for a short while, just after the pulling down of the Berlin wall. We had been so struck by the need in that land at that time. Shortly after that visit we were in Colorado, USA. Our daughter had recently given birth to our first grandchild and we had said we would bring home some American clothes for him. As we walked around the store looking at rack upon rack of clothes we remembered the sight we had seen in Poland: shop windows displaying just one dress, one baby bonnet and individual nappies. Confronted by the sight of so much in America we had found ourselves unable to buy anything. The contrast was so great. In that moment a second Robin Hood was born as Mike said,

"I believe God has called me to take the money from the pockets of the rich and put it into the pockets of the poor."

Our trip to Guatemala was the fulfilment, or at least a beginning, of that belief. Our past in America now became the present for the next years as we visited from time to time and spoke about what we had seen and shared the need. The Americans are generous people. God amazingly put all our past educational experience and our pastoring experience together so that we might use these gifts amongst these people.

On a subsequent visit to Guatemala Mike told me in an email that he had visited the city rubbish dump where a Christian work had been established some years before. Mike said that he would like to go to visit this work regularly and help in whatever way he could, but that it was not a place for me to go. I was SO relieved since I was to join him before long.

I arrived on Saturday, a free day for us. I had been there only a short while when Mike announced that we were to be picked up at mid-day on Monday to go to the Dump. Can you imagine my exclamation?

We drove through streets of utter poverty and eventually arrived. The broken down wooden door of The Potter's House stood before me, an armed guard outside, and some yards to the left was the rubbish dump. As we got out of the mini bus I was told to go quickly in and Mike handed me his handkerchief to put over my nose. I was horrified by all I saw. The lack of provisions and equipment, the squalor, the sight of such poor adults and ragged children, the vultures flying overhead, the disease, the food on their plates at lunch time. I could not eat. And yet the people who worked there called these folk who lived on the dump their treasures.

I could not wait for the time to pass so that we could go back to the comparative cleanliness of our home. But before we left Mike told them that we would come every Monday and Wednesday to help in whatever way we could. He had hugged and cuddled those children. I could only stand and watch him do it.

When we got back I went to my bedroom and cried for the rest of the day. I cried because I knew I could not go back there and therefore felt so guilty. Mike left me alone as I asked him to, coming in from time to time to see if all was well. Each time he came I sobbed louder. I remember so well such a tender moment when he wiped the tears from my cheeks with his handkerchief and said,

"One day God will do that for you."

As I wept I asked God to change my heart and several hours later I was able to go to Mike and say that I would go with him, if only to see what kind of woman could regularly do such a work (she had been away on my first visit). But I requested that we should go after lunch so that I did not have to witness the way they ate such awful looking food. Thus it was that I began to lead the staff in Bible studies, in English, whilst Mike taught the children and taught the teachers how to teach more effectively. How I came to love these children and some of their parents and the staff who valiantly worked there day by day. The numbers have since increased but at that time there were 650 people living on the dump. I mean *ON* the dump. I walked on it one day with the leader of the work. It would have been too dangerous to go alone. There were two taps for water and the people had to use them on a rota basis. Many of the children and adults were on drugs and were to be seen sniffing their glue. "Houses" were made from cardboard and polythene. Daily work for the people was to collect what garbage they could in order to sell it. Food was often found in the garbage that was dumped there. A baby slept in a too small cardboard box. How can you not be changed by such sights?

As we were leaving one of the dump homes the lady we had been visiting said that we could not leave with out taking a gift with us. She then proceeded to hand us some of the food that she had been preparing for the family meal. We tried to say that we did not need to take their food but she would not listen.

"God had blessed me," she said," I want to bless you."

I shall never forget watching little Farita and her friend playing with a small naked doll, no doubt cast aside by some child who had received a much nicer one. They laid a brick on the ground with another standing upright at the end of it. This became the doll's cot. What is your daughter's doll's cot like?

And so we became involved with these two major works in the city of Guatemala, an involvement which was to continue for some years. It was a place where we shed many tears. They have had their first graduate from the university who will become a doctor and four of the children from the dump have won scholarships to go and study in the States. How God has blessed the work of their willing hands.

A New Continent

We both attended the International meeting of the mission board when it met one year in Britain. We had been asked if we would host a South African couple for a week afterwards. At the conference Mike had been asked to speak about the work in Guatemala and he majored on the work of the school. People from all the continents were present at this time, but we were so surprised to discover that the couple from South Africa were black! We had expected a white couple! And so began a new experience for us.

After Mike had spoken the black couple joined us. Hendrick was overjoyed to have heard what Mike said had been achieved in the Guatemalan school.

"That is just the vision I have," he said. "Would you come to South Africa and talk to us about it?"

It was not many weeks later that we found ourselves on a plane bound for Johannesburg. The two hour drive from the airport to the black town of Siyabuswa was all I had ever expected Africa to be with its huge sky and horizon. I expected however, to see elephants outlined against the sky and these I did not see! Our weeks there passed so quickly. We visited many homes which had never had a white person within their walls. We spoke every evening of the Lord's goodness. I could not help, each time I spoke, asking the question,

"Why do you not hate us? We are white and your lives have been so dominated by whites in such a cruel way?"

"God has given us loving, forgiving hearts," was the reply I always received. This is surely the truth. How otherwise was a blood bath prevented? Nelson Mandela did such a wonderful job in the way he kept the peace in this country.

Again we saw such poverty but we were so impressed by the joy of the people. Pretty sang for us so beautifully. She is now with the Lord having been shot by her boyfriend.

Our visits to Africa continued for 6 years and developed to include Mozambique as the work done by Pastor Mahlangu grew like Topsy. But as the years passed we saw the increasing results of HIV Aids. Grave yards were full of many new graves. Almost every family lost members. Grandparents or just a grandmother would be in charge of maybe 10 of her grandchildren since all their parents had died. A whole generation is being wiped out and the later generation being infected.

We learned so much in this Africa. The need here is for money as in Guatemala. It is possible to buy most things in these countries but they have to have the money to do it. Homes are washed away in mud slides; 4000 died in one typhus epidemic and there is no money for medicine. People live without fresh water and with little food.

We were to visit Soweto. On the way Hendrick, who was driving, announced that we were going to stay in a squatter camp that night. I sat silently in the back of the van as I heard this.

"Lord, I have worked on the rubbish dump in Guatemala; do you really have to ask this of me as well? I cannot do it."

But I had no option since we were on our way and so yet again I found myself asking the Lord to change my heart, and that is what He did.

Our visit to Soweto taught me much about the apartheid years. We visited places with Ernest who had been a student during the riots in Soweto. He took us into a huge church. When the Afrikaner police had come out with their guns the students raced to the church to find refuge. But the police opened the doors and began to fire. The students lay on the ground to protect themselves but many of them were killed. Ernest wept as he showed us pictures of friends of his who had died at this time. On another occasion I saw this same young man raise his arms in praise with tears flowing as he looked at one of the country's most wonderful views. In the past the blacks had not been allowed to visit these beautiful places. They could only drive past. They were reserved for the whites.

We slept that night in the bed of the owners of the house. Holes were all over the corrugated roof and the bedclothes were sparse. Maria wept as we drank tea together saying,

"You are white and you are drinking from my cups. You are staying in my home."

What a privilege it was to do so; how honoured we were. It was a place I looked forward to re-visiting each time we subsequently visited Africa. God is able to change our hearts.

In our sixth year we both taught in the newly established Grace School. An orphanage was to be added to the school so that AIDS orphans could be cared for. The school has grown to over 600 pupils now. Having taught in Britain and been in American schools I could see the contrast so clearly. We casually cast books aside when they are deemed too old or we simply have to follow a new curriculum. Oh that we could find easy ways to transport books and materials to these places. Why do we not realise how blessed we are in this country and how much we have? Why are we not more spontaneously generous?

What a joy the children were in this school. Each morning they would be eagerly waiting for us to arrive and would then crowd round to carry our bags in to school for us. Bright shining eyes and big smiles. What a joy it was to teach in a truly Christian school. A problem of stealing occurred in one of the classes and so I sent both girls involved to the Head Mistress. They returned duly chastened and with goods restored. I was able to take them aside and talk to them about forgiveness as we sat on the steps outside the classroom. We prayed together, those small 7 year old girls and me! What more could one want? To be able to have a part in introducing the Gospel in such a vital way is truly wonderful.

One lad in my class never smiled. He was not very bright and so had difficulty in all subjects. It became my aim to see this child happy. I was so rewarded at the service held when we were leaving. This lad came to me and said,

"Thank you for teaching me to smile."

What a gift to receive.

Sitting at the dining table in our African home one evening we had some guests who had come to see the school. The subject turned to AIDS and one of them commented on how sad it was that one of the children in my class had this dreaded disease. I asked who it was and was told that it was this same lad whom I had taught to smile. My heart broke. He lives still at this moment but is often very ill.

Another Maria had given up her teaching job in order to collect up the children in her remote district who would never be able to afford to go to pre-school, a requirement in South Africa. When we first visited we saw a small corrugated shed into which were crammed 42 chairs. In the summer this was too hot and in the winter it was too cold. When activities took place half of the children would have to go outside to work unsupervised whilst Maria shared herself amongst them all. I photographed her as she returned from having fetched water for the children to drink. She walked gracefully despite the heavy bucket of water on her head. She had had to walk a long way to fetch this since they had no well or nearby water of any kind.

It is so good to see that generous gifts have enabled a pre-school to be built for over 80 children and a well now sits in their playground.

"Now we see in a glass darkly…"

Mission trips took us to other parts, not all of which I went to since my husband felt that some of them were too difficult. We did go to China together, but Haiti was for him alone. Such wonderful work is being done in the name of the Lord in these places, always in extreme circumstances.

Do you remember right at the beginning of this story I told you that we were enjoying living in a rut? Who would have believed that the Lord had all of this in store for us?

I must not let you run away with the idea that this was all star-shine and roses. Far from it. When Mike was preparing to go away by himself I would find the days leading up to that departure very difficult and I must admit to some resentment. I loved to be with him doing just ordinary things. However, I knew that if he were to go on his own he would be able to accomplish things he would not be able to do with me there. I saw clearly how the Lord was using him and was fully agreeable to his going. I would soon settle down into a routine after the unsettling of his departure. But then he would be returning again! I would be so excited at the prospect of his coming home, but when he arrived there would be another difficulty as I had to adjust to this. I know that this is not a very spiritual reaction but it is how things were for me and you deserve the truth. I could never see Mike giving up this work. He was characterised by great energy and enthusiasm which I could see going on until he was 90!

I have neglected to say that somewhere in amongst all of this we had moved house yet again. Including our childhood homes, our eleventh move. Amazingly it was back to our roots or almost our roots since it was back to the place we first lived in after we were married. Here we were back in the city where all our children had been born and where we had been so happy in our rut!

I was not too happy when Mike made the suggestion that we should move. After all, here I was beside the sea and I wanted to remain there. I knew that Mike preferred City life and therefore when he made this suggestion I questioned it. It had not come in isolation. Mike was the Chairman of a Chinese ministry and it was felt that they needed to move to a place of larger Chinese population. In looking for places to fulfil this need we discovered ourselves back in the city we had loved. But I needed to know that this was God's will and not Mike's. We were not at peace about it together.

One morning I walked, like Adam and Eve, in the garden in the cool of the day. As I walked amongst the trees in this garden I loved so much, I talked out loud to the Lord,

"Let me know that this is your will, if it be so, Lord."

I heard God answer me immediately,

"I have kept the best 'til last" He said.

"Yes, I know that you have kept the best until last" I replied, pointing up to heaven, "but do you mean that this move is the next step and that it is the last?"

I had no reply to this, but I immediately had peace and knew that it was OK to move. How do we know that it is God's voice? In the same way as we recognise the voice of a friend when we know each other well. It takes practise, and even then we are not always sure, at least, I am not always sure. The Holy Spirit within us convinces us, however.

Why did the Lord take us back to this place? We did not really know. I had been reluctant to leave the sea behind but the Lord had made it clear to me that this was His way for us and so here we were again, taking up friendships of nearly 40 years. How well I remember waking up the first morning in our new home. We had two windows in our bedroom. I chose to draw the curtains facing the bottom of our bed and was so surprised and disappointed to see the roof of the house next door and nothing else. I turned to the window my side of the bed which looked over the garden. As I drew those curtains my eyes were filled with the glorious splendour of two red oak trees at the bottom of our garden. They were a breath-taking sight. The Lord spoke to me again,

"Choose which window you look through".

I knew that applied to more than the simple opening of my curtains.

I must say that I looked forward greatly to the day when we might be able to settle down and live a more normal life, seeing the family much more often though two of our children were now overseas themselves. Our first years in this place were spent mostly in far away places for both of us. They were difficult in many ways because of this.

It was with great amazement that I heard Mike's words one day whilst we sat in the garden in South Africa. He had always said that he would know when the day had come that he did not want to step onto another aeroplane.

"I think the day has come when I should retire. When we go home I shall resign from the Mission Board."

He would actually be 65 years old just then, but this had nothing to do with age. This was the Lord speaking to him as clearly as He had done for many years.

Was this really going to happen? Again, there was no reason that was obvious to us, just that it would be right to finish at this time. Lord, can it really be?

We arrived home and sure enough his resignation was accepted.

What now? For the first time ever we could truly say that we had officially retired. It was a very strange experience. As we sat and prayed in our garden one day we came to the conclusion that the Lord would have us work with the passion that was in both our hearts for evangelism and discipleship. We would do that through friendship evangelism in whatever way the Lord led us. The bowls club, choirs, our neighbours; these were some of the areas the Lord led us into. I had the joy of leading an International Bible study each week. Post graduate students at the university in our city would often come to the country with their wives and these wives were the ones who came to this Bible study. Usually they were Chinese, Japanese or Korean. Very few of them were Christians and they came for a variety of reasons: to learn English, to see what our culture was like, or sometimes because they really wanted to know about the Bible. This has remained a constant joy. God brought these people to us instead of our having to go to their countries. What a privilege.

Constantly we had seen in our lives the working out of that favourite verse: "In all these things God works for the good of those who love Him………." We had experienced difficulties in many areas, some of which are not yet resolved, but enough for us to truly know the truth of this verse. We CAN trust Him though it may often be hard to do so.

Once again were blessed with great neighbours and some of these through the years have become good friends. One such couple lived over the road. They were going to be travelling to New York for a holiday and staying in Time Square. We asked them if they would go to David Wilkerson's church in Time Square and then come home and tell us all about it. This they did though Pastor David was ill, but they brought us as series of his tapes to listen to.

One of these tape series was called "Death of a Promise". Part one told us how God will often really test us when He does give us a promise, just as He did with Abraham and Sarah. The promise will seem to have become impossible to fulfil. This has to happen, he said, in order for us to see that it could only have been God who brought it to pass. With the ages of Abraham and Sarah when they gave birth to Isaac this must surely have been true! As Mike and I listened to this tape we stopped it after a short while so that we could recall promises that God had given to us through the years and therefore apply this sermon directly. For me the most recent had been when we had left the sea-side to come here to live. God had spoken to me quite clearly telling me that He had kept the best till last. That was what had given me peace about moving. Of course, many of His promises come straight from His word. But we need to see how they apply? Some of them are conditional I think.

Certainly I had often wondered during these early years of living here about the validity of having heard God say this. This was proving to be a most difficult time with our being apart so much. It did not seem to be "the best". But here in this sermon God was telling us that that promise had to die before it could be fulfilled. Now we were staying at home I wondered if we would now see that happen.

The second tape talked about the fact that God will often give us a window of opportunity and that we must make sure we do not miss it. He used the story of the Israelites travelling through the desert. They certainly missed their window of opportunity since only two of them were allowed to enter the Promised Land. I was fearful that I would miss an opportunity. During this sermon David Wilkerson mentioned the conclusion of the series would come that evening, but we only had two tapes. Where was the third? I contacted them and they kindly sent it to us. In this sermon we were reminded that God always keeps His promises, but were we willing to enter into His rest whatever the circumstances? This was more important than actually receiving the promise. Well, was I willing?

Death of that Promise

Having returned from Africa in August we were due to go to Brazil to see our son and our new grandson at the end of November on into December. What a thrill this was. Our family name was now going to continue. We all discovered unexpected joy in this fact. We had returned from Africa very tired and both of us had lost a lot of weight. Why is it that we women always recover this weight loss so quickly? I did. But Mike did not. Also he had remained very tired. Whilst in Brazil he found eating very difficult, something he always excelled in during our travels with his willingness to try anything and to help me out very often!

We returned from Brazil and went to our daughter for Christmas. Mike continued to be tired, so much so that I had been saying that he must visit the doctor after Christmas.

What a wonderful doctor we had! He made it easy for Mike to return to him as often as we felt necessary to sort out what we felt may be a bug he had picked up in foreign parts. But the day came when Mike returned with the words,

"He has referred me to the lymphoma clinic."

A type of leukaemia was suspected. An MRI scan followed this visit and together we went to hear the results. Gently the consultant told us that unfortunately it was not leukaemia which might have been able to be treated. Instead, it was kidney cancer, for which there was very little that could be done. Treatment was available but it was known that it had a very small success rate.

How did we leave the hospital that day and drive home? I do not know. I cannot remember. I do know that Peter and Selma were at home when we arrived. I shook my head as I entered through the gate and saw them sitting in the garden.

"It's not good", I said.

We told them the news and wept together there in each others arms.

Peter and Selma were here with little Danny and consequently we were to have a family celebration of being together for the first time in 12 years. We had been so looking forward to this time. How different it was going to be now. In fact Mike went into hospital for the first time and was released just 2 days before we were all to be together for the weekend. Family photos were able to be taken for which we were so grateful. The first time we were to be together after such a long time…….and the last time ever. Oh Lord, how could this be?

I recall being with a friend and crying so bitterly whilst saying that I did not feel we had very long left. In fact, we had exactly one year.

I kept a diary during this time, an occasional diary recording facts and feelings. I regularly sent out emails under the heading "update" and was often comforted by the replies from friends.

I do not know what to say here really. My memory seems to be flawed since I seem to find it impossible to remember things exactly. What did we talk about? How did we pray? I remember weeping together. I remember Mike saying that he did not want to die because I had so many times said that I would never be able to manage without him. My reply to that was that he had always told me that God would take care of me much better than he could himself and so he had no need to worry. Wow! How that answer must have come from God, not from me! I did not FEEL that. I just said it.

Some moments stand out very clearly, however. At the hospital one time when he had again been admitted as an emergency (was it not always so?), our pastor took me aside.

"May I ask you a difficult question?" he asked.

I took a long time to answer him knowing that I would not be terribly happy with his question, whatever it was. But I answered,

"Yes."

"Are you willing to let Mike go?"

My reply was to sob out my answer,

"No."

How could I be willing for God to do this: to take my husband whom I loved so dearly and could not face being without? Pastor went on to say that unless I could get to that point he felt that we would miss much joy that the Lord would have for us in this situation.

He must have said much the same to my daughter because the next day, at the hospital, as we sat with Mike, she suddenly began to talk about a funeral. Tears flowed from the three of us but we began to make plans and in the next two days completely planned the thanksgiving service we would have.

We laughed as Mike joked about things and we read together 2 Corinthians Chapter 4 which Mike said he would like to be read.

A few days earlier our other daughter had told us that her youngest child had asked if she could say a sermon for Grampa. Finding something to be a lectern, at the age of 7 she read the whole of Psalm 139 to the rest of the family. When we told Mike he exclaimed that we must read that at the service for this little one. In fact, the four children read some verses each. A precious moment.

Was there joy in all of this? I honestly do not know. What I DO know is that when Mike had died I was SO glad that we had done all this planning together and so I knew we would be doing exactly what Mike wanted. This was a burden that we did not have to bear and I would suggest to everyone that they should talk about such things when all is well so that guesses do not have to be made.

When Mike died hundreds of cards and letters came. All of them, and when I talked with people, would say how wonderful it was that Mike knew God; that I knew where he was now; that God was comforting me. Endlessly did such comments come but I did not experience the truth of any of them. One of the first questions I asked my pastor immediately after Mike's death while we were still with him, was,

"Where is Mike now?"

I had never questioned that before. I was always ready with the obvious answer. But this was different. Where was he? I was no longer sure. In the coming days I combed the scriptures to see what they had to say about death. I knew it all in my head. I knew the scriptures, but suddenly I needed to know more and could find no satisfaction.

I craved being on my own with the exception of being with the family. During this whole year, and subsequently, I have learned more than ever before, the value of the family. It is beyond price.

I listened to Mike's sermons on tape. I played favourite pieces of music, especially our favourite of all favourites, Neil Diamond's "Hello My friend." Over and over again. Was it hard to do this? Unbelievably so, but I had to do it. Some one told me that I must stop running to other people for comfort, that I must find it in God alone. How wrong they were. For one thing I did not go to others. I preferred to be alone, much to the distress of those who wanted to be with me. But when I did venture forth, when I found the energy and strength to meet with a good friend, I found the release of tears, difficult though that was, and their sharing of my grief a balm to my soul. What a blessing that God does not leave us on our own but that He gives us those to share our joys and sorrows with.

I could see Mike in the pulpit. I could see him in those last few minutes of his life but I could see him in no other situation. As I write I still find that to be so. I cannot find Mike anywhere. I cannot hear him as I walk or imagine him coming into a room. Sometimes I speak to him,

"Hello. Would you like some tea?"

Or

"Thank you for this cup of coffee".

"Come into the garden with me."

Isn't it silly? Yet I do it still. Sometimes in bed I pretend to wrap my legs around his and entwine my feet with his and even put my arm around him or ask him to put his around me. But it does not happen. People sometimes say "He is always with you." No. He isn't. That's the trouble."

But this was not a crisis of faith. Words are difficult to find. I did not question God. I was not angry with Him. All I could say was that it was not what I had ever expected. Had this really happened to me? It was not possible. We were Mike and Mary, "the M and M's" as Mike would often say (some of his favourite sweets!) There could be no one of us on their own. I knew that God's ways are not our ways, and I am so glad about that. I would not want His ways to be the same as mine. But.......

In his book "A Grief Observed", C.S. Lewis comments that when his wife died it was as if his faith had been a house of cards and that it had collapsed. Later he says that if it WAS a house of cards, then it needed to collapse in order to be re-built. I identified with every word in this book. In fact it was the only one of several which were then given to me which made any sense at all. I read it and re-read it. I can never lend it to anyone since it is underscored many times over. It became so precious.

Here was the only one who thought as I did. My faith did not collapse, but it has changed radically. Things to which I have always had answers have now become a mystery to me. In fact, the whole of my faith has become more and more of a mystery. It has become greater. I believe that God knows what He is doing……….

Whilst Mike was ill I discovered Isaiah 57 verses 1 and 2 which comforted us a great deal and continue to do so.

After Mike had died I received a beautiful little framed text reminding me that God cares for the broken hearted. I have discovered that he does. But it took a while for me to get there.

"In all these things………..." This has been the biggest test of my faith ever. Can there ever be anything larger than this? I believed that my life had also ended with Mike's death. I felt as if I had lost my identity since I realised that for so many years my life had been so inextricably bound up with Mike's. My identity was his also. Without him I was lost. What about those plans that God tells me in Jeremiah that He has for me? I felt that there could not be any plans left for me. But at the same time I knew that God's word just had to be true still. I have not yet discovered what these plans are but I do believe that they are in place. I just have to wait for them to be revealed.

I have learned so much. I have discovered what wonderfully faithful friends God has given to me. Some have dropped by the wayside, maybe because they have seen me only in relation to Mike and without him there is nothing. This has been a shock to discover.

I have also discovered that we all react in different ways to the same event. One friend of mine hates to be alone now that her husband has died. I have to be alone for much of the time. Some feel that their husbands are near them. I do not. I have learned that most people do not know how to react to tears. Others clearly feel that after a year the bereaved one is OK to get on alone. Others, however, remember dates that are so important and send cards or telephone with their love. What a joy that is. But I miss the cuddles, the hugs. The telling me that he loves me.

I have learned what is it to be utterly alone and lonely; to cry out to God for comfort and find that He gives it. That He takes those tears and those cries and sits with me, holding my hand.
There are so many tears in this world. I pray that I might become more sensitive to them in knowing how to comfort.

Yesterday I listened to a sermon on television. David Jeremiah related a happening the conclusion of which was that he told the lady who had come to him for counsel, whose husband had left her, that there was much more to life than marriage. That God still had life for her to live. I think I had been guilty of thinking that there really is no life for me outside marriage. I can see that now. And so, God, I wait for you to give me a dream. I wait to see where you will lead me. I believe that even in this, even in this, you will work for my good because I do love you with all my heart.

A New Beginning

On July 4th 2007 I moved from Southampton to Sheffield to live near Kathie and family. That was a good date to choose, wasn't it? Independence Day! This idea had come to me one day and I had asked the Lord to confirm it. A few weeks later I had gone to stay with them and Kathie had asked me if I ever considered moving up to be near them. Life changed gear in that moment as we began immediately to look for bungalows. I was not running away from Southampton. True I found it difficult to see so many things and places which constantly reminded me that Mike was not there. This was especially so in the garden where we would spend so much time together. I knew that it would be alright if I stayed. But it did seem a good time to move whilst I was still young enough (?) to make an independent life for myself.

Had I known how traumatic the year would be after deciding to move, I would never have done it. Again, what a blessing that we are not aware of the future. I left friends, church and home and trusted that God would look after the future for me. He is doing that though I cannot say it is easy. But I find it easier for me to be in a place where I do not have memories of Mike all the time. For some this would be the last thing they would want, but for me it is right.

How strange life is. It is almost as if Mike has never been. I cannot explain it. I have learned/am learning to live on my own and am finding it much easier now than I had ever thought it would be.

I am blessed with great neighbours and a church in which I am finding my way. Friendships are growing. But, oh, how long this takes. I have discovered my own identity and have become just plain "Mary". No longer the two of us. I cry seldom these days. But my heart aches somewhat when I see couples holding hands as we used to do. Though I am also so glad to see others doing the same!

Am I glad I moved? Was it really God's idea rather than my own? I wonder sometimes but then I think that shows a real lack of faith. He has never let me down in the past and will not do so now

"Do not have false expectations," Mike would say.

And he would be right. And so, rightly, I have begun to carve out a life for myself which is independent of the family but highly dependent on relationships with people. I know I need them and some of them seem to need me.

Sometimes, Lord, I have glimpses of you having kept the best till last when my heart is flooded with joy. You are teaching me to "take every thought captive". How often I have to do that. You are teaching me to "be content whatever the circumstances" How difficult that is. But when I eventually realise that I am in a situation which demands that I look at one or the other of those verses and then when I apply it, peace comes.

I want my life to be consecrated to you, Lord. I want to discover that you truly are my bridegroom and to have that love for you which surpasses all else. I want to be filled with you so that you overflow all the time and others may see you. I want to introduce others to you and to help people grow in their knowledge of you along with me. I am free to do this being on my own in a way I have never been able to do before. Lead me on, Lord, please.

    I need your companionship. I need your comfort. I need your leading and so much more. You must be my everything.

Acknowledgements

Many people are mentioned in this story but not by name. To every one of them I offer my grateful thanks for their part in helping me through my life to discover more of my Lord.

And to Him alone be praise!

Made in the USA
Charleston, SC
10 February 2013